D0119151

Old English Sheepdogs

Stephanie Finne

Checkerboard
Library

An Imprint of Abdo Publishing
www.abdopublishing.com

www.abdopublishing.com

Published by Abdo Publishing, a division of ABDO, PO Box 398166, Minneapolis, MN 55439. Copyright © 2015 by Abdo Consulting Group, Inc. International copyrights reserved in all countries. No part of this book may be reproduced in any form without written permission from the publisher. Checkerboard Library™ is a trademark and logo of Abdo Publishing.

Printed in the United States of America, North Mankato, Minnesota.
102014
012015

Cover Photo: Alamy
Interior Photos: Alamy pp. 19, 21; Corbis p. 11; Glow Images p. 15; iStockphoto pp. 1, 5, 7, 9, 13, 17

Series Coordinator: Tamara L. Britton
Editors: Megan M. Gunderson, Bridget O'Brien
Production: Jillian O'Brien

Library of Congress Cataloging-in-Publication Data

Finne, Stephanie, author.
  Old English sheepdogs / Stephanie Finne.
      pages cm. -- (Dogs)
  Audience: Ages 8-12.
  Includes index.
  ISBN 978-1-62403-676-7
  1. Old English sheepdog--Juvenile literature. 2. Working dogs--Juvenile literature. I. Title.
  SF429.O4F56 2015
  636.737--dc23
                              2014025409

Contents

The Dog Family

Old English sheepdogs are one of more than 400 dog **breeds**. Where did all those dogs come from? Scientists believe dogs evolved from the gray wolf. So like wolves, dogs are part of the family **Canidae**.

Wolves are successful hunters. Early humans noticed this and wanted to use these skills on their own hunts. So more than 12,000 years ago, humans tamed wolf pups to help them hunt.

Like wolves, dogs were good hunters. Eventually, humans bred dogs for other jobs. Some dogs became protectors and companions. The Old English sheepdog was bred to herd livestock.

The Old English sheepdog

Old English Sheepdogs

The Old English sheepdog's beginnings are lost to history. However, the Old English sheepdog was developed in western England. The **breed** can be traced back to the early 1800s.

Like other herding and droving dogs, Old English sheepdogs have **docked** tails. This led to the nickname bobtail. The Old English sheepdog is still known by that name today.

In 1888, the first Old English sheepdog was registered with the **American Kennel Club (AKC)**. Soon, the breed was popular with wealthy Americans. In 1904, the Old English Sheepdog Club of America was formed.

By the 1970s, the **breed** was popular with pet owners. However, many did not realize the amount of grooming an Old English sheepdog's coat needs. Over time, the number of **AKC** registered Old English sheepdogs declined. By 2013, the breed was ranked number 78 with the AKC.

A 2007 law banned tail docking in England. So today, Old English sheepdogs in their ancestral home have long tails.

What They're Like

Old English sheepdogs are happy dogs with an even nature. They love to play and want to be part of the family. These social dogs should not be left alone or in a crate for long periods of time.

These intelligent dogs were **bred** to herd livestock. So, they think for themselves. This can make training difficult. But, Old English sheepdogs love attention. Ignoring bad behavior and praising good behavior can make training easier.

Old English sheepdogs are energetic. They will even herd family members that are scattered around the house! If you want a fun, high-energy dog, the Old English sheepdog is the pet for you.

Exercise gives the active Old English sheepdog the mental and physical stimulation it needs.

Coat and Color

Old English sheepdogs have a double coat. The harsh-textured outer coat is waterproof. It resists rain. The dog's body is **insulated** from cold weather by a thick **undercoat**. The double coat keeps the dog warm and dry in winter weather.

In warmer weather, the Old English sheepdog will **shed** its undercoat. To avoid **mats**, the dog must be groomed every day or two. This is very important. A matted coat may cause skin problems.

The Old English sheepdog's coat can be any shade of gray, or blue. It can also be blue **merle**. In addition, the coat can be **grizzled**. These colors can appear with or without white markings. The Old English sheepdog's eyes can be blue or brown. Some have one eye of each color!

Some Old English sheepdog owners reduce coat grooming requirements with the short "pet cut."

Size

The Old English sheepdog is a strong and muscular **breed**. Males are 22 inches (56 cm) and taller and weigh 70 to 90 pounds (32 to 41 kg). Females are slightly smaller. They stand 21 inches (53 cm) or taller and weigh 60 to 80 pounds (27 to 36 kg).

The Old English sheepdog's body is well muscled. The square head has a strong jaw. Medium-sized ears are flat to the head. The **muzzle** is square and short and ends with a black nose.

From the head, a long, graceful neck leads to a short, compact body. The body is broader at the rear end than it is at the shoulders. It rests on muscular legs that end in small, round paws. In the United States, the Old English sheepdog's tail is **docked**. In other countries, the tail may be its natural length.

A male Old English sheepdog is larger than a female.

Care

Old English sheepdogs require an annual exam with a veterinarian. As a dog gets older, it will need to see the vet more often.

During this visit, the vet will check the dog's health and give it any necessary **vaccines**. He or she will also **spay** or **neuter** dogs that will not be **bred**.

A dirty coat can hold body waste and fleas. So along with regular grooming, the Old English sheepdog needs an occasional bath. Bath time is a good opportunity to trim the dog's nails and clean its ears. Brushing the dog's teeth each day helps prevent tooth decay and gum disease.

Overweight Old English sheepdogs can have joint trouble or **diabetes**. So, an Old English sheepdog will need a lot of exercise. Daily walks or play in a fenced yard are important. Proper care results in a happy, healthy dog.

Regular exams are a critical part of a dog's lifetime health maintenance. Its relationship with the vet is an important one.

Feeding

An important part of an Old English sheepdog's care is a quality diet. Feeding once or twice a day is most common. Puppies need to eat more often.

An Old English sheepdog needs big, sturdy food and water bowls. These should always be clean. A stand to lift the bowls up off the floor can make it easier for the big dog to eat.

There are different types of dog food. Dry foods help clean the dog's teeth. Semimoist foods are softer and do not need to be refrigerated. Canned foods are moist, but they spoil quickly.

Choose a food that is labeled "complete and balanced." This means it contains all the **protein** and **nutrients** a dog needs. And, be sure to provide clean, fresh water every day.

All dogs love treats!
Be sure to keep a
proper portion size to
avoid weight gain.

Things They Need

Aside from proper food and health care, an Old English sheepdog has other needs. A dog that needs much exercise will also need a collar and a leash. An identification tag will help your dog get home if it becomes lost. A vet can also insert a **microchip** in your pet.

In order to properly care for the coat, grooming tools are a must. Brushes, combs, and clippers will keep the coat clean and free of **mats**. At bath time, shampoo made for dogs will not irritate eyes and ears.

Finally, your Old English sheepdog should have a crate. The crate will provide a safe place that feels like a den. A crate is a good place for an Old English sheepdog to go to relax.

A crate is the safest place for a
dog to be when traveling.

Puppies

After mating, a female Old English sheepdog is **pregnant** for about 63 days. There are usually four to eight puppies in a **litter**.

Newborn puppies are helpless. They are born blind and deaf and they cannot walk. They depend on their mother for everything. The puppies spend their time sleeping and drinking their mother's milk.

When puppies are two weeks old, their eyes start to open. Two weeks later, the puppies can see, hear, and play. When they are 8 to 12 weeks old, the puppies are ready for a good home.

Have you decided an Old English sheepdog is the right dog for your family? If so, find a reputable **breeder**. Good breeders will know the history of their dogs. They will make sure the puppy is healthy and has had its **vaccines**.

Puppies are born black and white. Their color lightens as they grow.

Old English sheepdog puppies quickly become balls of energy. It is important to begin training and **socializing** your puppy right away. A healthy, well cared for Old English sheepdog will be a loving companion for 10 to 12 years.

Glossary

American Kennel Club (AKC) - an organization that studies and promotes interest in purebred dogs.

breed - a group of animals sharing the same ancestors and appearance. A breeder is a person who raises animals. Raising animals is often called breeding them.

Canidae (KAN-uh-dee) - the scientific Latin name for the dog family. Members of this family are called canids. They include wolves, jackals, foxes, coyotes, and domestic dogs.

diabetes - a disease in which the body cannot properly absorb normal amounts of sugar and starch.

dock - to cut short, especially a tail or ears.

grizzled - a coat on which hair is tipped with silver, gray, or white.

insulate - to keep something from losing heat.

litter - all of the puppies born at one time to a mother dog.

mat - a tangled mass.

merle - having dark patches of color on a lighter background.

microchip - an electronic circuit placed under an animal's skin. A microchip contains identifying information that can be read by a scanner.

muzzle - an animal's nose and jaws.

22

neuter (NOO-tuhr) - to remove a male animal's reproductive glands.

nutrient - a substance found in food and used in the body. It promotes growth, maintenance, and repair.

pregnant - having one or more babies growing within the body.

protein - a substance which provides energy to the body and serves as a major class of foods for animals. Foods high in protein include cheese, eggs, fish, meat, and milk.

shed - to cast off hair, feathers, skin, or other coverings or parts by a natural process.

socialize - to adapt an animal to behaving properly around people or other animals in various settings.

spay - to remove a female animal's reproductive organs.

undercoat - short hair or fur partly covered by longer protective fur.

vaccine (vak-SEEN) - a shot given to prevent illness or disease.

Websites

To learn more about Dogs, visit **booklinks.abdopublishing.com**. These links are routinely monitored and updated to provide the most current information available.

Index